Wild Savannah Zoos

written by Lucinda Cotter

Engage Literacy is published in 2013 by Raintree.
Raintree is an imprint of Capstone Global Library Limited, a company
incorporated in Engand and Wales having its registered office at 7 Pilgrim
Street, London, EC4V 6LB – Registered company number: 6695582
www.raintreepublishers.co.uk

Originally published in Australia by Hinkler Education, a division
of Hinkler Books Pty Ltd.
Text and illustration copyright © Hinkler Books Pty Ltd 2012

Written by Lucinda Cotter
Lead authors Jay Dale and Anne Giulieri
Illustrations on pp 4, 10, 14, 16, 18 by Cherie Zamazing
Edited by Gwenda Smyth
UK edition edited by Dan Nunn, Catherine Veitch and Sian Smith
Designed by Susannah Low, Butterflyrocket Design

Wild Savannah Zoos
ISBN: 978 1 406 26513 2
10 9 8 7 6 5 4 3 2

Printed and bound in India

Acknowledgements
Cover images (left to right): © Mark Eastment | Dreamstime.com; Fairfaximages/Andrew De La Rue;
© Amgphotography | Dreamstime.com; p5 top left: © Ghm Meuffels | Dreamstime.com; p5 top right
(and back cover): © Roman Murushkin | Dreamstime.com; p5 main: Lonely Planet Images/Tom Cockrem;
p5 bottom: © Rosa Furtado | Dreamstime.com; p6 top left: © Vernerf | Dreamstime.com; p6 top right:
© Oleg Znamenskiy | Dreamstime.com; p6 bottom: © Sefi Greiver | Dreamstime.com; p7 top left:
iStockphoto.com/ © Ricardo De Mattos; p7 top right (and Contents page bottom): © Mark Eastment |
Dreamstime.com; p7 middle left: © Photomyeye | Dreamstime.com; p7 middle right: © Federicoriz |
Dreamstime.com; p7 bottom left: © Atakhar | Dreamstime.com; p7 bottom right: iStockphoto.com/ © ©
Graeme Purdy; p8 top left: iStockphoto.com/ © Olga Zaytseva; p8 top right: iStockphoto.com/ © Ranplett;
p9 bottom left: Getty Images/AFP/Stringer; p9 bottom right: Cyril Ruoso/ JH Editorial/ Minden Pictures;
p10 bottom left: Lonely Planet Images/Dennis Johnson; p11 top left (and Contents page top): © Karen
Graham | Dreamstime.com; p11 top right: © Isselee | Dreamstime.com; p11 middle left: © Sam D'cruz
| Dreamstime.com; p11 middle right: © Miercuri | Dreamstime.com; p11 main: © Amgphotography |
Dreamstime.com; p12: © Peripitus; p13 top (and title page): Fairfaximages/Andrew De La Rue; p13 bottom
left: Fairfaximages/Justin McManus; p13 bottom right: Fairfaximages/Angela Wylie; p15 top left: Deb
Olson, Taronga Zoo; p15 top right: © Newspix/News Ltd/Nathan Edwards; p15 middle right: Photograph
by Mark James, courtesy Taronga Western Plains Zoo; p15 bottom left: Photograph by Rick Stevens, courtesy
Taronga Western Plains Zoo; p17(all): African Lion Safari, Cambridge, Ontario, Canada; p18 inset:
© Markuso53 | Dreamstime.com; p19 main: © Stickpen; p19 top left: Fotosearch/SuperStock; p19 top
right: © Arthurrh; p19 middle right: © Johannes Gerhardus Swanepoel | Dreamstime.com; p19 bottom
right: © Neal Cooper | Dreamstime.com; p20 (both): Zoological Society of San Diego; p21: Courtesy Kelly
Landen, www.elephantswithoutborders.org; p23 top: Getty Images/Image Source; p23 middle left: © Maigi
| Dreamstime.com; p23 middle right: Ambient Images Inc./SuperStock; p23 bottom: iStockphoto.com/
© Narelle Robson-Petc

Contents

What Is a Savannah?

A savannah is grassland — a place with very few trees, but lots of grass. Savannahs are found in places where it is warm all year round. They have a wet season (warm with lots of rain) and a dry season (warm with very little rain).

The African savannah is an area between the *rainforest* and the *desert*.

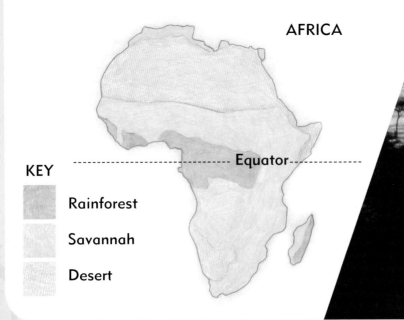

AFRICA

------------------------------------- Equator --------------

KEY

Rainforest

Savannah

Desert

Animals of the Savannah

The savannah is home to many different animals. Lions, elephants, cheetahs, giraffes and zebras live in the African savannah. So do rhinoceroses, gazelles, meerkats, wildebeests and many more.

Cheetah

Elephant

Giraffe

Wildebeests

Meerkat

Lion

Rhinoceros

Zebra

Gazelle

Some animals of the savannah are now *endangered*. This means they are in danger of dying out. These animals are endangered because of hunting, and because their *habitats* have been *destroyed*. People have damaged the savannah through *cattle grazing, pollution* and lighting fires.

Hunters kill animals such as African elephants, black rhinoceroses and cheetahs for their skin or other body parts. These animals are now almost *extinct*. Extinct means that the animals have all died; there are no more left in the world. That is why much of the African savannah has been made into special *wildlife parks* where the animals that are left are *protected* and safe.

Rhinoceroses' horns

Elephants' tusks

Serengeti National Park

The Serengeti National Park is one of Africa's best-known wildlife parks. It covers a very large area in Tanzania. People are not allowed to live in the Serengeti National Park.

The Serengeti National Park is home to many animals that are endangered. The black rhinoceros is almost extinct after being hunted for its horns. *Park rangers patrol* the park day and night to protect the rhinoceroses from *illegal* hunters called poachers.

AFRICA

KEY

Tanzania

Serengeti National Park

Park ranger

In the past, poachers hunted African elephants for their *ivory tusks*. In 1990, there were only 500 African elephants left in this area. Today, ivory is not allowed to be sold; and thanks to the work of the park rangers, there are now over 2,100 elephants in the park.

Cheetahs, African wild dogs and even lions are also endangered animals. They, too, are protected in the Serengeti National Park.

Zoos Around the World

Other countries around the world are helping to save and protect the animals that live in the African savannah. One of the ways these countries help is by making their own safari parks. A safari park is made to look like the savannah in Africa and is a safe place for endangered animals. When people go to safari parks they can learn all about African animals.

In this book, you will read about three very special safari parks.

Taronga Western Plains Zoo

The Taronga Western Plains Zoo in Australia is a very large safari park. It is home to over 1,000 animals and is the only zoo in Australia where *visitors* can see African elephants and black rhinoceroses.

Visitors can walk around the zoo's many paths, or explore the zoo by car, bike or *electric cart*. They can even stay overnight — sleeping in tents and going on a night *safari*.

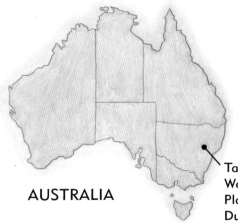

AUSTRALIA

Taronga Western Plains Zoo, Dubbo

The zookeepers from this zoo work with groups of people around the world who are saving endangered animals. One of the animals they are trying to save is the African black rhinoceros. Eleven black rhinoceroses have been born at the Taronga Western Plains Zoo.

African Lion Safari

In Canada there is a safari park called the African Lion Safari. Visitors can drive through the large zoo full of lions, zebras, ostriches and giraffes. The park also has a boat that takes visitors around a lake, as well as a train that takes them close to the animals.

The zoo has a special breeding programme for Asian elephants and cheetahs. A breeding programme is where the baby animals are born in a safe place. A large number of elephants and cheetahs have been born at the zoo.

KEY

Canada

United States of America

African Lion Safari

San Diego Zoo Safari Park

In the United States of America, there is a special safari park called the San Diego Zoo Safari Park. Lots of African animals roam freely in this zoo. The zoo has its own African *village*, and there is an *aviary* for birds and an animal hospital.

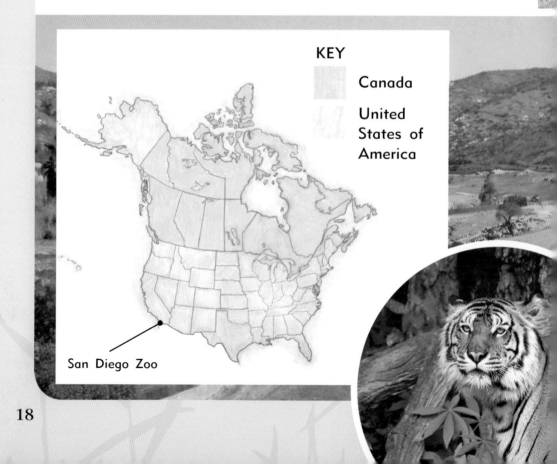

KEY

Canada

United States of America

San Diego Zoo

There are two unusual ways to explore this safari park.

Flightline

Visitors who want a thrill can 'fly' over the park on a *cable* with a seat attached.

Rolling Safari

Another way to see the zoo is by riding a two-wheeled electric cart called a Segway. On a Segway, people can go off the track and explore the park.

The San Diego Zoo Safari Park works with a group of people in Africa who are trying to protect African elephants. This group of people follow herds of elephants to watch how they live. If you are interested in this work, you can go to a special website to see the elephants and what they are doing.

What Can You Do to Help?

Even though Africa may be a long way from your home, there are many things you can do to help protect endangered animals and their habitats.

YOU COULD:

→ Protect animal habitats near your home by joining clean-up days and always leaving wildlife in their habitat.

→ Offer to help the nearest zoo or wildlife park and learn about its work.

→ Learn about endangered animals and share this information with your friends.

There is so much more to know about open-range zoos. Why don't you explore the four zoos in this book by visiting their websites?

Glossary

aviary: a place where birds are kept

cable: very strong steel rope

cattle grazing: cows eating grass

desert: a dry place with very little rain

destroyed: hurt, damaged or ruined

electric cart: a small cart that uses electricity to move

endangered: in danger of dying out

extinct: died out, gone forever

habitats: the places where animals live

illegal: not allowed

ivory tusks: the very long, large teeth coming out from an elephant's mouth

park rangers: men and woman whose job is to look after animals in a protected area

patrol: to move around, keeping watch

pollution: litter on land; smog in the air; oil and waste in water

protected: looked after, safe

rainforest: a rainy place with large trees and plants

safari: a special trip to look at wild animals

village: a very small town

visitors: people who go to see someone or something

wildlife parks: places where animals are protected

Index